I'M NOT YOUR YOUR MOTHER

Helen Rice

First published in Great Britain by Written Off Publishing, 2024
Copyright © Helen Rice, 2024
The moral right of the author has been asserted.

Author photograph © barkaphotography.co.uk

Written Off does not use AI.

ISBN: 978-1-915320-40-7

Written Off Publishing
Owley Wood Road
Weaverham
Cheshire
CW8 3LF

writtenoffpublishing.com

Edited by Rebecca Kenny at Written Off
Cover art © Edie McCartney, @theartistedie

Printed in the UK using recycled materials by Mixam Ltd.

Dedicated to all those who do (or have done) some mothering.

CONTENTS

Look   9
The Stepchild   10
I'm Trying   11
Passing   12
Bath Time   13
Lockdown Fish Tank   14
Saturday Kitchen   15
At the School Gates   17
My Goblin Angels   18
Other People's Babies   20
Buns   21
If you'd have been   22
Carrying Weight   23
High Shelves   24
Here's a thing you can do   25
Washing the toys   26
The Unconsoled   27
Tea bags   28
Lockdown Fish   29
I've made you a mousemat   30
Nanny State   32
When I lived here before   33
Advice on Surviving 'Stepmum Saturday'   34
Split Crystals   35
Shall I be mother?   36
What Is This Tie That Binds?   38
Love is (parts one and two)   39

Acknowledgements / About the Author   41
About Written Off   48

I'M NOT YOUR MOTHER

LOOK

I know this isn't perfect
I know this isn't 'family life'
as refracted through the fucked-up lens
of late-capitalist marketing
but you can't dispute
that since I moved in
at least there's always loo roll.

THE STEPCHILD

the child comes to me fully formed
I cannot mould him
like his dad
I must love him just as he is
or not at all

I'M TRYING

    to be a stepmum
But I don't know what to do
There's no nine-month incubation
There's nobody to coo

There's no ante-stepmum classes
There's no soothing belly rub
No bespoke yoga lessons
There's no stepmum 'in the club'

There's no stepchild shower parties
No appropriate greetings card
To mark this graduation
From girlfriend. It's just hard.

PASSING

some days I can pass

maybe it's the scraped-back hair
or maybe I get the tone of
"will you PLEASE stop doing THAT!"
exactly right
or maybe, most likely, they just assume

like that flat-packed May Sunday in the park
when a cautious dad adds
"check with your mum first"
after offering you some of his kids' crisps

and you don't correct him
and you don't reject me
and you look to me and I nod assent

and it feels like acceptance
and it feels like a 'moment'

and then your chubby fingers
encrusted with barbeque beef dust
stuff a grab-bag fistful of reconstituted potato
into your face
and I think maybe
most likely
you just really, really wanted

some crisps

BATH TIME

I take baths instead of showers in this place
In this house where you've lived a separate life
After struggling to carve myself some space
I take baths instead of showers in this place
You absorb my suggestions with good grace
Even handing me the tools; the spade, the knife
I take baths instead of showers in this place
In this house where you've lived a separate life

LOCKDOWN FISH TANK

There are countless jobs to complete
But you've spent the day making a fish tank
There are clothes everywhere in heaps
But you've spent the day making a fish tank

There are paving slabs left uncut, despite talk
But you've spent the day making a fish tank
The dog's scratching the door, desperate for a walk
But you've spent the day making a fish tank

There's a truculent child we're supposed to teach
There's shopping to do, under rules we can't breach
There's the relentless piles of bills and admin
Another meal to conjure from packet and tin
There's an elderly mother who needs visiting
And those songs that we really should be rehearsing
But you've spent the day making a fish tank

There's a stack of books left unread
There's a hundred things we should be doing instead

You have spent the day making a fish tank
That fits perfectly at the end of the bathtub
So that at the end of another day of unticked lists
We can lie back in the bath together
And breathe
And watch the fish

SATURDAY KITCHEN

As I tackle another tower of
dirty plates
at the sink
you
enter

a NERF gun in each hand and another strapped to your back

BANG BANG BANG BANG

BANG BANG BANG BANG

BANG

BANG BANG

BANG BANG BANG BANG BANG BANG BANG BANG BANG

BANG BANG

BANG

and as you gleefully sprint to your bedroom
to re-arm with more foamy ammo
I plunge rubber gloves back into warm suds
fish out a soft pellet and
place it by the dripping pots

I smile
and say to an empty room

I really love this quality time we get to spend together

AT THE SCHOOL GATES

"Well mine, after she's had her tea,
she just gets into her pyjamas
And puts herself to bed!"

"Well mine, after he's had his tea, he tidies away all his toys, and
then he just gets into his pyjamas
And puts himself to bed!"

"Well *mine*, after she's had *her* tea, she tidies away *all* her toys,
then she hoovers the entire house

And then she just gets into her pyjamas
And puts herself to bed!"

.....Well.....

....*mine*....

emits a special gas that makes everyone in a 15-mile radius feel
slightly better about their lives.

MY GOBLIN ANGELS

On a bad day
you sulk.
Show me up.
Bash branches with some rusting shears we found
while litter-picking the park bushes.

I carefully hold used needles at long distance
popping them into the sharps bin
alongside mounting black bags
containing a cornucopia of condom wrappers
endless shards of broken vodka bottles,
crisp packets and knock-off Red Bull cans.

When are we going home?
When are we going home?
When are we going home?

Once home you moan you're bored
Daddy's house is boring; no Xbox, no telly, no Wi-Fi
no snacks except the fruit bowl

I neck gin from a can while making the food
that none of you want to eat
and watch the clock tick slowly towards
my freedom fagbreak.

On a good day
you text me from Morrisons, "Do you want anything?"
you remembered your ID
you return with wine to soothe my Saturday aches
I think
'This is the flip side'
this is the bonus I reap
for another woman's sore nipples
another woman bled for you
I raise my glass of red to you, and toast her
for my goblin angels

on a good day
I'm the glory hunter
sucking up the joy and celebration
I'm sneaking in at the end of the show
soaking up the encore
whispering, 'How did it go?'

OTHER PEOPLE'S BABIES

I am so sick of making things for other people's babies I am so sick of knitting and stitching for other people's babies I am so sick of hearing about other people's babies I am so sick of hearing other people's babies I am so sick of holding other people's babies I am so sick of holding the small hands of other people's babies as we cross the road to school I am so sick of other people's babies telling me what they want to be when they grow up and I am so sick of watching other people's babies grow up I am so sick of other people's babies growing up into wonderful independent vibrant human beings I am so sick of loving other people's babies I am so sick of other people's babies asking "didn't you ever want to have babies Auntie Helen?"

BUNS

I'm cleaning another woman's oven
because she's got a bun in the oven
toxic chemicals you see
whereas I'm the spare branch on the tree
oh lovely, thoughtful, expendable me

IF YOU'D HAVE BEEN

you'd have been fifteen
on your last birthday

If you'd have been
you'd have been seen on the screen
when they pressed down hard on my jellied belly
belly bean

But a belly bean that never was
wasn't there

I walk away from the clinic
in the loose-fitting trousers they told me to wear
bought especially
feeling confused
and free
and utterly empty

CARRYING WEIGHT

On the morning of her miscarriage
you knew you were feeling hopeless
and in need of solace
when you walked into a crystal shop
in mist-mired November Bridlington.
Left with two (paid-for) coloured lumps in your coat pockets
one for her, one for you.
Yellow calcite,
hardsmoothmilkyellow.

The wannabe witches behind the counter
say, "It increases strength and motivation,
it will improve self confidence and hope,
it will help heal grief and
it will bring comfort in tougher times."
So you buy them and carry them next to your hips
all week.
Even though neither of you really believe
in that magic rocks shite.
You both just needed something solid
to
     hold
          on
            to.

HIGH SHELVES

I wish I had a grown-up son
he wouldn't have to come round often
but he'd be someone I could call on
he could help me change the light bulbs
take my wool down from the high shelves
he wouldn't have to come round often

and he's awful busy with his work
and his family, and his clubs
but he could help me change the light bulbs
take my wool down from the high shelves
I wish I had a grown-up son
he wouldn't have to come round often
but he'd be someone I could call on

HERE'S A THING YOU CAN DO

go to the house of a man you once knew
a man you think you could have loved

hold the new son
another woman has borne him
try to look as happy for them
as you say you are

and know that she is better for him
than you would have been

WASHING THE TOYS

She said, "I washed it all out of love"
He said, "You've washed all the love out of it"

THE UNCONSOLED

through the thick curtains of your unwashed
hair I can smell the unhappiness

you silently slide the console remote towards me
no words required for this familiar transaction

I hook my nail in the tiny groove and
shoogle the spent batteries out

pointedly placing them in my special tin
marked 'old batteries for recycling'

 I snip open a new packet with the second-best kitchen scissors
and an unmistakable flourish:
box-fresh double AAs

the remote slips back
into your boy-man hands

you grunt and I choose to believe this is some kind of thanks

I'll see you in a couple of hours when you need feeding

TEA BAGS

You meticulously pick every
scrap of organic roast
aubergine from your portion
of homemade moussaka
exclaiming,
"It's like chewing on a used tea bag!"
and I say through tight teeth,
"That's a very inventive use of simile,
well done."

LOCKDOWN FISH

He says, "What fish shall we get next?"
I say, "I think maybe we have enough fish for now."
The third tank in as many weeks has appeared in the house in
the living room this time

and he tells me there is a calculation you can do
measuring length of fish
to surface area of tank

and I think about how much space we need to live
and I think about how much space we need to thrive
and I wonder what sort of life do we wish
for our fish.

I'VE MADE YOU A MOUSEMAT

with a picture of the dog on it.
I'm picturing you, alone, in halls
As mid-term approaches.

Are you warm enough?
Are you wearing clean clothes?

I don't know what you'll be eating
but I can guess. It's not good is it.
I'm picturing you in seminars
being asked to speak.

What does a sentence coming out of your mouth sound like?

I'm picturing you with essays to write at your computer.
You must be able to write essays or
you wouldn't be there.
I've never read them. I'd like to.
I'm picturing you in the evening
in a new city.

Have you been out yet?
Have you been socialising?
Have you made any friends or
are you just playing online games?

I'm picturing you at some kind of event
on your course, enforced,
in a shirt collar a bit too tight,

checking your phone
constantly
looking for the soonest opportunity to leave.

I've made you a mousemat
with a picture of the dog on it
because I know you like the dog.

NANNY STATE

"I do not believe in nationalising children"
Brendan Clarke-Smith, Member of Parliament for Bassetlaw
21 October 2020

I'm not your mother
but when you need a hand to hold
hold mine

I'm not your mother
but when you're getting another cold
I'll get those posh tissues you like
and forego tonight's gin

I'm not your mother
but when your parents
are tired and broke and hungry
you need to know you can count on me

I'm not your mother
and I don't have to be
to want you to learn
with a full belly

I'm not your mother
but one needn't be a mother
to do some mothering

WHEN I LIVED HERE BEFORE

    I would wander through the shopping centre
and touch the tiny clothes of
the babies I would never have,
the bibs and bonnets
and the wee shoes.

Who knew
something so small could kick so hard?

ADVICE ON SURVIVING 'STEPMUM SATURDAY'

try not to interpret
 the scrunched damp hand towel
  on the bathroom floor
   as a microaggression
    when you pick it up
     and place it
    over the radiator

 for the fourteenth fucking time that day
sometimes a scrunched damp hand towel on the bathroom floor
is

  just

   a

    towel

SPLIT CRYSTALS

All week you have pestered by WhatsApp for us to make a recipe you've seen on TikTok. A hideous concoction of sugar, corn syrup and blue food colouring designed to mimic crystal meth in candy form. I repeatedly explain that corn syrup 'isn't really a thing' in England and try to refrain from elaborating on the history of US farm subsidies even though there's a bit of my ego impressed I remember this from studying A-Level politics twenty years before you were born. I'm also suppressing my irritation at the constant use of 'candy' instead of 'sweets', reminding myself that your grandparents might have winced at the use of 'sweets' instead of 'spice'.

We improvise with agave and, somewhat inevitably, it doesn't set properly. A whole shelf of the fridge is devoted to this flavourless, azure, too-gooey toffee. Having spent the afternoon contentedly crafting boxes and baggies in which to flog our 'product' to your pals, you leave pissed-off and need prompting to wish me goodbye.

Will you remember the fun of the making? Will you appreciate that I went ingredient shopping when all I really wanted to do was curl up in the unmade bed of my own self pity? How I bought you a beanie hat with my last fiver so you could look like Jesse? Stood supervising your stirring so you didn't splash yourself with sticky lava? Downloaded the Breaking Bad playlist on Spotify for maximum atmosphere?

Or will you just recount closing the fridge door on our failure?

Today I will force myself into the kitchen again. Resplit the doomed gloop with water and reboil. Trying to get the sweet hard crackle right this time. Hoping to make you happy.

SHALL I BE MOTHER?

The cramps and first few spots of blood
that Christmas morning confirm
my most longed-for present is absent, again
I shall not be mother today
maybe next month.

The grip of her tiny hand in mine
as we cross the road for her first day of nursery
"Is she yours?" They ask at the door,
"No." Her mum is over there
taking her other, more nervous, child to his first day of big school
I shall not be mother today
but I help them out when they're busy.

Watching you climb a park frame designed to be hard
encouraging you not to give up and return
to the familiar safety of the toddler-friendly playground
but to stay here and risk falling, promising that I will hold on
and keep watching
and help you up
and it'll be worth it
it'll be worth it because, "You'll feel so good when you make it to
the top, and you are going to make it to the top, and then we'll be
able to tell Daddy all about it!"

After some stumbles and scrapes and with much prompting
you manage it
stand proud on the bolted ropes like
you were born to mount them.

I shall not be mother today
though I do actually feel like one, a bit.

You grin broadly and shout with excitement,
"Take a picture to show Mummy!"

My phone is already in hand
anticipating this demand
I've been recording your ascent throughout
I open the messaging app
and press *send*.

WHAT IS THIS TIE THAT BINDS?

I watch you drive away in the car your dad has patched up
laden with that particular late teenage mix of textbooks
way beyond my ken, childhood toys and
grown-up lingerie. A very great deal of very grown-up lingerie.

This past three months I have laundered more
lingerie than I have ever owned.
Fancy, flimsy, stringy, skimpy
unsubstantial and unscaffolded.
My middle-aged bosom holders dry alongside
trying not to tut.

Your mum wanted you to "take it to a proper garage"
and — somewhat against my better judgement —
I convinced you to "trust him, just this once..."

No Wharton's Jelly ever set between us
yet here I am
my nest bereft of another bird's chicks
missing you
finding your shed feathers in the sink
orange peel under the settee
a desiccated apple core wedged beneath the bedroom door.

Collecting them all
as compost to nurture my garden.

LOVE IS (1)

the polyester fibres of my fleece dressing gown tie
wiping the tears from your cocoa-stained face
after you have been crying for a solid seven minutes
into your duvet
because I did a sinister Scottish voice while reading *Harry Potter
and the Prisoner of Azkaban*
and you absolutely did not like it

LOVE IS (2)

two pairs of surprisingly pert middle-aged buttocks
touching throughout an unseasonably cold spring night
with the perfect weight of a small ginger dog
evenly spread
over our four aching middle-aged feet

THE END

ACKNOWLEDGEMENTS

Success has many mothers and this small pamphlet of words is no exception. I would like to acknowledge and thank the following people.

The Wise Talk Programme, tutors and participants and particularly The Wise Talk Collective of Chris Singleton, Camille McCawley and Sonia Burns for their boundless support. I could not have done this without you.

Several of these poems began life in poetry workshops. Thanks to the organisers and participants of Papercrane Poets, Sunday Wordship, Brave Words, Herding Cats and the Writers Workshop for giving me space to create.

Those who helped me refine and edit my work (in addition to those mentioned above): Leanne Moden, Sophie Sparham and Helen Mort.

The spoken word scene of the Midlands and the North, in particular Wordwise of Derby, which gave me my first experience of spoken word, and the many nights in Sheffield which have supported my progress. Thanks especially to Stan Skinny for taking a chance on me.

The teachers at Portway Junior and Woodlands Community School who inspired a love of reading, writing, poetry and performance from an early age, particularly Mrs Gibbins and Mr Whycherley.

Finally, John and 'the kids' and 'the kids' mums' who let me be part of their lives (and write about it).

Thank you, Hx

ABOUT THE AUTHOR

Photo by barkaphotography.co.uk

Helen Rice is a writer and performer based in Sheffield. In 2019, Helen was one of six poets chosen for the Wise Talk performance development programme, an Arts Council England-funded project for emerging artists living and working in or around Sheffield. She won first prize at Leeds Poetry Festival's national poetry competition in 2022 and was published in their anthology 'Taking Up Space'. In addition to poetry and spoken word Helen creates comedy and music. Her un-paean to the pandemic screen-dominated life, 'I don't wanna Zoom with you', was selected by the BBC to be preserved in the British Library digital archive of 'art made by the community during COVID-19'. Helen's various art forms and forthcoming gigs are represented on her website.

https://helenriceisshowingoff.com

ABOUT THE PUBLISHER

Written Off is a publishing company founded in and run from the North of England. It came into existence after Founder Rebecca Kenny's arrival home from hospital following a car crash in which she broke her neck, back, pelvis, sternum and sacrum. Its logo, an open umbrella, acts as a symbol of change, new starts, risk and taking a chance on the unknown.

Having her car written off, her career written off, and then being somewhat written off herself, Rebecca chose the company's name with an aim to reclaim power from adversity and show that just because society maintains a status quo, that doesn't mean you can't make waves.

Written Off do not charge for submissions, we do not charge to publish and we make space for writers who may struggle to access traditional publishing houses, specifically writers who are neuro-divergent or otherwise marginalised. We never ask anyone to centre their trauma, and we like to champion authentic voices.

All of our beautiful covers are designed by independent queer artists. Please do take the time to follow their work.

Find us online at writtenoffpublishing.com